50 Pudding & Custard Recipes for Home

By: Kelly Johnson

Table of Contents

- Classic Vanilla Pudding
- Chocolate Custard
- Rice Pudding
- Butterscotch Pudding
- Lemon Curd
- Crème Brûlée
- Chocolate Pudding
- Banana Pudding
- Mango Pudding
- Coconut Rice Pudding
- Pistachio Pudding
- Chia Pudding
- Creme Caramel
- Baked Custard
- Bread Pudding
- Coconut Custard
- Raspberry Pudding
- Rice Pudding with Cinnamon
- Vegan Chocolate Pudding
- Eggless Vanilla Custard
- Tapioca Pudding
- Pumpkin Custard
- Avocado Chocolate Pudding
- Mocha Pudding
- Maple Pudding
- Rhubarb Custard
- Strawberry Vanilla Pudding
- Vanilla Bean Custard
- Panna Cotta
- Lemon Meringue Pudding
- Orange Pudding

- Caramel Custard
- Blueberry Pudding
- Almond Pudding
- Matcha Custard
- Chocolate Hazelnut Pudding
- Cherry Custard
- Pear and Ginger Pudding
- Spiced Rice Pudding
- Coffee Pudding
- Peanut Butter Custard
- Fig Pudding
- Carrot Cake Custard
- Apple Cinnamon Pudding
- Cinnamon Custard
- Banana Custard
- Brown Sugar Custard
- Chocolate Mint Pudding
- Raspberry Custard
- Coconut Mango Pudding

Classic Vanilla Pudding

Ingredients:

- 2 cups (480ml) whole milk
- 2 large egg yolks
- ¼ cup (50g) sugar
- 1 teaspoon vanilla extract
- 2 tablespoons cornstarch

Instructions:

1. **Mix Ingredients:** Whisk together milk, egg yolks, sugar, and cornstarch in a saucepan.
2. **Cook:** Heat over medium heat, stirring constantly until it thickens (about 5-7 minutes).
3. **Cool:** Remove from heat, stir in vanilla, and refrigerate for 2 hours.

Chocolate Custard

Ingredients:

- 2 cups (480ml) heavy cream
- ½ cup (100g) sugar
- 2 tablespoons cocoa powder
- 2 large egg yolks
- 1 teaspoon vanilla extract

Instructions:

1. **Heat Cream & Cocoa:** In a saucepan, heat cream and cocoa powder over medium heat until hot but not boiling.
2. **Mix with Egg Yolks:** Whisk together sugar and egg yolks in a bowl, then pour the hot cream mixture into the eggs while whisking.
3. **Cook:** Return to saucepan, cook on low heat, stirring until it thickens. Remove from heat and stir in vanilla. Chill before serving.

Rice Pudding

Ingredients:

- 1 cup (200g) Arborio rice
- 4 cups (960ml) whole milk
- 1 teaspoon vanilla extract
- ¼ cup (50g) sugar
- ½ teaspoon ground cinnamon

Instructions:

1. **Cook Rice:** In a saucepan, bring milk and rice to a simmer, cook for about 25 minutes until rice is tender.
2. **Sweeten & Flavor:** Stir in sugar, vanilla, and cinnamon, cook for another 5 minutes until thickened.
3. **Serve:** Allow to cool and serve warm or chilled.

Butterscotch Pudding

Ingredients:

- 2 cups (480ml) whole milk
- 1 cup (200g) brown sugar
- 3 tablespoons unsalted butter
- 2 tablespoons cornstarch
- 1 teaspoon vanilla extract

Instructions:

1. **Melt Butter & Sugar:** In a saucepan, melt butter and brown sugar over medium heat until bubbly.
2. **Add Milk & Cornstarch:** Stir in milk and cornstarch, cook until thickened (about 5 minutes).
3. **Finish:** Remove from heat, stir in vanilla, and refrigerate for 2 hours before serving.

Lemon Curd

Ingredients:

- 1 cup (240ml) lemon juice
- 1 tablespoon lemon zest
- 1 cup (200g) sugar
- 4 large egg yolks
- ½ cup (120g) unsalted butter, cubed

Instructions:

1. **Whisk Ingredients:** In a saucepan, whisk together lemon juice, zest, sugar, and egg yolks.
2. **Cook:** Over medium heat, cook while stirring constantly until thickened.
3. **Add Butter:** Remove from heat, stir in butter, and refrigerate for 2 hours before serving.

Crème Brûlée

Ingredients:

- 2 cups (480ml) heavy cream
- 5 large egg yolks
- ½ cup (100g) sugar
- 1 teaspoon vanilla extract
- ¼ cup (50g) sugar for caramelizing

Instructions:

1. **Preheat Oven:** Preheat to 325°F (160°C).
2. **Mix Cream & Eggs:** Heat cream until hot, then whisk in egg yolks and sugar. Stir in vanilla.
3. **Bake:** Pour mixture into ramekins, bake in a water bath for 30-40 minutes. Chill for 2 hours.
4. **Caramelize:** Sprinkle sugar on top and caramelize with a torch or broil until golden brown.

Chocolate Pudding

Ingredients:

- 2 cups (480ml) whole milk
- ½ cup (100g) sugar
- ¼ cup (25g) unsweetened cocoa powder
- 2 tablespoons cornstarch
- 1 teaspoon vanilla extract

Instructions:

1. **Mix Ingredients:** Combine sugar, cocoa powder, cornstarch, and milk in a saucepan.
2. **Cook:** Cook over medium heat until thickened, whisking constantly (about 5 minutes).
3. **Chill & Serve:** Stir in vanilla and refrigerate for 2 hours before serving.

Banana Pudding

Ingredients:

- 2 cups (480ml) whole milk
- 1 cup (240ml) heavy cream
- ½ cup (100g) sugar
- 3 large egg yolks
- 2 tablespoons cornstarch
- 1 teaspoon vanilla extract
- 2 ripe bananas, sliced

Instructions:

1. **Cook Pudding:** Combine milk, cream, sugar, egg yolks, and cornstarch in a saucepan. Cook over medium heat until thickened.
2. **Assemble:** Layer pudding, banana slices, and vanilla wafers in a dish. Chill for 2 hours.

Mango Pudding

Ingredients:

- 2 cups (480ml) coconut milk
- 1 cup (200g) mango puree
- 3 tablespoons sugar-free sweetener
- 2 tablespoons agar agar powder

Instructions:

1. **Cook Mango & Coconut Milk:** In a saucepan, combine mango puree and coconut milk, bring to a simmer.
2. **Add Agar Agar:** Stir in sweetener and agar agar, cook for 5 minutes.
3. **Chill:** Pour into molds and refrigerate for 2 hours before serving.

Coconut Rice Pudding

Ingredients:

- 1 cup (200g) Arborio rice
- 2 cups (480ml) coconut milk
- 1 cup (240ml) whole milk
- ¼ cup (50g) sugar-free sweetener
- ½ teaspoon vanilla extract

Instructions:

1. **Cook Rice:** Bring rice, coconut milk, and whole milk to a simmer and cook until rice is tender (about 20-25 minutes).
2. **Sweeten & Flavor:** Stir in sweetener and vanilla, cook for an additional 5 minutes.
3. **Serve:** Allow to cool or serve warm.

Pistachio Pudding

Ingredients:

- 2 cups (480ml) whole milk
- ½ cup (50g) shelled pistachios
- ¼ cup (50g) sugar
- 2 tablespoons cornstarch
- 1 teaspoon vanilla extract

Instructions:

1. **Blend Pistachios:** Blend pistachios with a bit of milk until smooth.
2. **Cook Pudding:** Combine pistachio mixture, sugar, cornstarch, and remaining milk in a saucepan.
3. **Thicken & Chill:** Cook until thickened, then refrigerate for 2 hours before serving.

Chia Pudding

Ingredients:

- 2 tablespoons chia seeds
- 1 cup (240ml) almond milk
- 1 teaspoon vanilla extract
- 1 tablespoon sugar-free sweetener

Instructions:

1. **Mix Ingredients:** Combine chia seeds, almond milk, vanilla, and sweetener in a bowl.
2. **Chill:** Refrigerate for at least 4 hours or overnight to allow it to thicken.

Crème Caramel

Ingredients:

- 1 cup (240ml) heavy cream
- 1 cup (240ml) whole milk
- 3 large eggs
- ½ cup (100g) sugar
- 1 teaspoon vanilla extract
- ¼ cup (50g) sugar for caramel

Instructions:

1. **Make Caramel:** In a saucepan, heat sugar until it melts and turns golden. Pour into ramekins.
2. **Prepare Custard:** Whisk together cream, milk, eggs, sugar, and vanilla.
3. **Bake:** Pour custard over caramel and bake in a water bath at 325°F (160°C) for 40 minutes. Let cool and refrigerate before serving.

Baked Custard

Ingredients:

- 2 cups (480ml) whole milk
- 4 large eggs
- ¼ cup (50g) sugar
- 1 teaspoon vanilla extract
- ¼ teaspoon ground nutmeg

Instructions:

1. **Mix Ingredients:** Whisk together milk, eggs, sugar, vanilla, and nutmeg.
2. **Bake:** Pour into a baking dish and bake at 350°F (175°C) for 30-35 minutes or until set.

Bread Pudding

Ingredients:

- 4 cups (200g) cubed stale bread
- 2 cups (480ml) whole milk
- 2 eggs
- ¼ cup (50g) sugar
- 1 teaspoon cinnamon
- 1 teaspoon vanilla extract

Instructions:

1. **Prepare Bread:** Place cubed bread in a baking dish.
2. **Mix Custard:** Whisk together milk, eggs, sugar, cinnamon, and vanilla, then pour over bread.
3. **Bake:** Bake at 350°F (175°C) for 45 minutes until golden and set.

Coconut Custard

Ingredients:

- 1 can (400ml) coconut milk
- 2 large eggs
- ¼ cup (50g) sugar
- 1 teaspoon vanilla extract
- ¼ teaspoon ground cinnamon

Instructions:

1. **Mix Ingredients:** Whisk together coconut milk, eggs, sugar, vanilla, and cinnamon.
2. **Bake:** Pour into a baking dish and bake at 350°F (175°C) for 30-35 minutes.

Raspberry Pudding

Ingredients:

- 2 cups (240g) fresh raspberries
- 1 cup (240ml) whole milk
- 2 tablespoons sugar-free sweetener
- 2 tablespoons cornstarch
- 1 teaspoon vanilla extract

Instructions:

1. **Cook Raspberries:** Heat raspberries in a saucepan until they break down into a puree.
2. **Prepare Pudding:** Mix milk, sweetener, and cornstarch, and add to the raspberry puree. Cook until thickened.
3. **Chill:** Remove from heat, stir in vanilla, and refrigerate before serving.

Rice Pudding with Cinnamon

Ingredients:

- 1 cup (200g) Arborio rice
- 4 cups (960ml) whole milk
- ¼ cup (50g) sugar
- 1 teaspoon cinnamon
- 1 teaspoon vanilla extract

Instructions:

1. **Cook Rice:** Simmer rice in milk over medium heat until rice is tender (about 25 minutes).
2. **Sweeten & Flavor:** Stir in sugar, cinnamon, and vanilla, cook for another 5 minutes.
3. **Serve:** Serve warm or chilled.

Vegan Chocolate Pudding

Ingredients:

- 1 ½ cups (360ml) almond milk
- ¼ cup (50g) unsweetened cocoa powder
- 2 tablespoons cornstarch
- ¼ cup (60ml) maple syrup
- 1 teaspoon vanilla extract

Instructions:

1. **Whisk Ingredients:** Combine almond milk, cocoa powder, cornstarch, and maple syrup in a saucepan.
2. **Cook:** Heat over medium heat, whisking constantly until it thickens (about 5-7 minutes).
3. **Cool:** Remove from heat, stir in vanilla, and chill before serving.

Eggless Vanilla Custard

Ingredients:

- 2 cups (480ml) whole milk
- ¼ cup (50g) sugar
- 2 tablespoons cornstarch
- 1 teaspoon vanilla extract

Instructions:

1. **Mix Ingredients:** Whisk together milk, sugar, and cornstarch in a saucepan.
2. **Cook:** Heat over medium heat, stirring constantly until thickened.
3. **Chill:** Remove from heat, stir in vanilla, and refrigerate for 2 hours before serving.

Tapioca Pudding

Ingredients:

- ½ cup (90g) small tapioca pearls
- 2 cups (480ml) whole milk
- ¼ cup (50g) sugar
- 1 teaspoon vanilla extract

Instructions:

1. **Soak Tapioca:** Soak tapioca pearls in water for 30 minutes.
2. **Cook Pudding:** In a saucepan, combine milk, sugar, and tapioca. Cook on low heat until thickened (about 20-25 minutes).
3. **Serve:** Stir in vanilla and refrigerate before serving.

Pumpkin Custard

Ingredients:

- 1 cup (250g) pumpkin purée
- 1 cup (240ml) whole milk
- 2 eggs
- ¼ cup (50g) sugar
- 1 teaspoon cinnamon
- 1 teaspoon vanilla extract

Instructions:

1. **Mix Ingredients:** Whisk together pumpkin purée, milk, eggs, sugar, cinnamon, and vanilla.
2. **Bake:** Pour into a baking dish and bake at 350°F (175°C) for 30-35 minutes until set.

Avocado Chocolate Pudding

Ingredients:

- 2 ripe avocados
- ¼ cup (60ml) unsweetened cocoa powder
- 2 tablespoons sugar-free sweetener
- 1 teaspoon vanilla extract
- ¼ cup (60ml) almond milk

Instructions:

1. **Blend Ingredients:** Combine all ingredients in a blender and blend until smooth.
2. **Chill:** Refrigerate for at least 30 minutes before serving.

Mocha Pudding

Ingredients:

- 1 ½ cups (360ml) almond milk
- 2 tablespoons instant coffee granules
- 2 tablespoons unsweetened cocoa powder
- ¼ cup (50g) sugar
- 2 tablespoons cornstarch
- 1 teaspoon vanilla extract

Instructions:

1. **Heat Ingredients:** In a saucepan, combine almond milk, coffee, cocoa powder, sugar, and cornstarch.
2. **Cook:** Heat over medium heat, stirring constantly, until thickened.
3. **Cool & Serve:** Stir in vanilla, chill for 1-2 hours, and serve.

Maple Pudding

Ingredients:

- 2 cups (480ml) whole milk
- ¼ cup (60ml) maple syrup
- 2 tablespoons cornstarch
- 1 teaspoon vanilla extract

Instructions:

1. **Mix Ingredients:** Whisk together milk, maple syrup, and cornstarch in a saucepan.
2. **Cook:** Heat over medium heat, whisking constantly until thickened.
3. **Chill:** Remove from heat, stir in vanilla, and refrigerate for 2 hours before serving.

Rhubarb Custard

Ingredients:

- 2 cups (480ml) whole milk
- 1 cup (250g) rhubarb, chopped
- ½ cup (100g) sugar
- 2 large eggs
- 2 tablespoons cornstarch

Instructions:

1. **Cook Rhubarb:** In a saucepan, simmer rhubarb with sugar and a splash of water until softened.
2. **Prepare Custard:** Whisk together eggs, milk, and cornstarch, then add to the cooked rhubarb.
3. **Cook & Serve:** Cook on low heat until thickened, then refrigerate for 2 hours before serving.

Strawberry Vanilla Pudding

Ingredients:

- 2 cups (480ml) whole milk
- 1 cup (150g) fresh strawberries, pureed
- ¼ cup (50g) sugar
- 2 tablespoons cornstarch
- 1 teaspoon vanilla extract

Instructions:

1. **Cook Pudding:** Whisk together milk, pureed strawberries, sugar, and cornstarch in a saucepan.
2. **Heat:** Cook over medium heat until thickened.
3. **Chill:** Stir in vanilla, refrigerate for 2 hours before serving.

Vanilla Bean Custard

Ingredients:

- 2 cups (480ml) heavy cream
- 1 vanilla bean, split and scraped
- 4 large egg yolks
- ½ cup (100g) sugar

Instructions:

1. **Heat Cream & Vanilla:** In a saucepan, heat cream with vanilla bean until hot, but not boiling.
2. **Mix Eggs & Sugar:** Whisk together egg yolks and sugar, then slowly add hot cream to the yolks.
3. **Cook Custard:** Return to saucepan, cook on low heat until thickened. Strain and chill for 2 hours before serving.

Panna Cotta

Ingredients:

- 2 cups (480ml) heavy cream
- 1 cup (240ml) whole milk
- ¼ cup (50g) sugar
- 1 teaspoon vanilla extract
- 1 tablespoon gelatin

Instructions:

1. **Dissolve Gelatin:** In a small bowl, dissolve gelatin in a bit of warm water.
2. **Heat Cream & Milk:** In a saucepan, heat cream, milk, and sugar until sugar dissolves.
3. **Combine & Chill:** Stir in dissolved gelatin and vanilla, pour into molds, and refrigerate for at least 4 hours.

Lemon Meringue Pudding

Ingredients:

- 2 cups (480ml) whole milk
- ¼ cup (50g) sugar
- 2 tablespoons cornstarch
- 3 large egg yolks
- 1 teaspoon lemon zest
- ¼ cup (60ml) lemon juice
- 3 egg whites
- ¼ cup (50g) sugar for meringue

Instructions:

1. **Prepare Pudding:** Whisk together milk, sugar, cornstarch, egg yolks, lemon zest, and lemon juice.
2. **Cook:** Cook over medium heat until thickened.
3. **Meringue:** Beat egg whites with sugar until stiff peaks form, then top the pudding with meringue.
4. **Bake:** Bake at 350°F (175°C) for 10-12 minutes until golden brown.

Orange Pudding

Ingredients:

- 2 cups (480ml) whole milk
- ¼ cup (50g) sugar
- 2 tablespoons cornstarch
- 1 teaspoon orange zest
- ¼ cup (60ml) orange juice
- 1 teaspoon vanilla extract

Instructions:

1. **Mix Ingredients:** Whisk together milk, sugar, cornstarch, orange zest, and orange juice.
2. **Cook:** Cook over medium heat, stirring constantly, until thickened.
3. **Chill:** Stir in vanilla and refrigerate for 2 hours before serving.

Caramel Custard

Ingredients:

- 1 cup (240ml) whole milk
- 1 cup (200g) sugar
- 2 large eggs
- 1 teaspoon vanilla extract

Instructions:

1. **Make Caramel:** In a saucepan, melt sugar until it turns golden brown, then pour into ramekins.
2. **Prepare Custard:** Whisk together milk, eggs, and vanilla, then pour into ramekins over the caramel.
3. **Bake:** Bake in a water bath at 350°F (175°C) for 30-40 minutes. Let cool and refrigerate before serving.

Blueberry Pudding

Ingredients:

- 1 cup (150g) fresh blueberries
- 2 cups (480ml) whole milk
- ¼ cup (50g) sugar
- 2 tablespoons cornstarch
- 1 teaspoon vanilla extract

Instructions:

1. **Cook Blueberries:** Simmer blueberries in a saucepan until soft and juicy.
2. **Prepare Pudding:** Whisk together milk, sugar, and cornstarch, add to blueberries, and cook until thickened.
3. **Chill:** Remove from heat, stir in vanilla, and refrigerate for 2 hours before serving.

Almond Pudding

Ingredients:

- 2 cups (480ml) almond milk
- ¼ cup (50g) sugar
- 2 tablespoons cornstarch
- 1 teaspoon almond extract
- 1 teaspoon vanilla extract

Instructions:

1. **Mix Ingredients:** Whisk together almond milk, sugar, and cornstarch in a saucepan.
2. **Cook:** Heat over medium heat, whisking constantly until thickened.
3. **Flavor:** Stir in almond and vanilla extracts.
4. **Chill:** Refrigerate for 2 hours before serving.

Matcha Custard

Ingredients:

- 2 cups (480ml) whole milk
- 2 tablespoons matcha powder
- 3 large egg yolks
- ¼ cup (50g) sugar
- 1 teaspoon vanilla extract

Instructions:

1. **Heat Milk & Matcha:** Warm milk and matcha powder in a saucepan until hot.
2. **Whisk Eggs & Sugar:** In a bowl, whisk together egg yolks and sugar.
3. **Combine:** Slowly pour hot milk into egg mixture while whisking, then return to the saucepan.
4. **Cook:** Heat on low until thickened, then stir in vanilla.
5. **Chill:** Refrigerate for 2 hours before serving.

Chocolate Hazelnut Pudding

Ingredients:

- 2 cups (480ml) whole milk
- ¼ cup (50g) sugar
- 2 tablespoons unsweetened cocoa powder
- ¼ cup (60g) hazelnut butter
- 2 tablespoons cornstarch
- 1 teaspoon vanilla extract

Instructions:

1. **Mix Ingredients:** Whisk together milk, sugar, cocoa powder, hazelnut butter, and cornstarch in a saucepan.
2. **Cook:** Heat over medium heat, stirring constantly, until thickened.
3. **Flavor:** Stir in vanilla extract.
4. **Chill:** Refrigerate for 2 hours before serving.

Cherry Custard

Ingredients:

- 2 cups (480ml) whole milk
- 1 cup (150g) fresh cherries, pitted and chopped
- ¼ cup (50g) sugar
- 2 large egg yolks
- 2 tablespoons cornstarch
- 1 teaspoon vanilla extract

Instructions:

1. **Cook Cherries:** Simmer cherries in a saucepan with a little water until softened.
2. **Prepare Custard:** Whisk together milk, sugar, egg yolks, and cornstarch.
3. **Combine:** Slowly pour the milk mixture into the cherries, cook until thickened.
4. **Chill:** Stir in vanilla and refrigerate for 2 hours before serving.

Pear and Ginger Pudding

Ingredients:

- 2 cups (480ml) whole milk
- 1 pear, peeled and grated
- 2 tablespoons sugar-free sweetener
- 2 tablespoons cornstarch
- 1 teaspoon grated fresh ginger
- 1 teaspoon vanilla extract

Instructions:

1. **Cook Pear & Ginger:** In a saucepan, simmer grated pear with ginger for 5 minutes.
2. **Mix Ingredients:** Whisk together milk, sweetener, and cornstarch, then add to the pear mixture.
3. **Cook:** Heat over medium heat, stirring constantly until thickened.
4. **Chill:** Stir in vanilla and refrigerate for 2 hours.

Spiced Rice Pudding

Ingredients:

- 1 cup (200g) Arborio rice
- 4 cups (960ml) whole milk
- ½ cup (100g) sugar
- 1 teaspoon cinnamon
- 1 teaspoon nutmeg
- 1 teaspoon vanilla extract

Instructions:

1. **Cook Rice:** Bring rice and milk to a simmer and cook for 25 minutes until rice is tender.
2. **Sweeten & Flavor:** Stir in sugar, cinnamon, nutmeg, and vanilla, then cook for 5 more minutes.
3. **Serve:** Allow to cool or serve warm.

Coffee Pudding

Ingredients:

- 1 ½ cups (360ml) coffee, brewed strong
- 2 cups (480ml) whole milk
- ¼ cup (50g) sugar
- 2 tablespoons cornstarch
- 1 teaspoon vanilla extract

Instructions:

1. **Mix Ingredients:** Combine coffee, milk, sugar, and cornstarch in a saucepan.
2. **Cook:** Heat over medium heat, stirring constantly, until thickened.
3. **Chill:** Remove from heat, stir in vanilla, and refrigerate for 2 hours.

Peanut Butter Custard

Ingredients:

- 2 cups (480ml) whole milk
- ¼ cup (50g) sugar
- 3 tablespoons peanut butter
- 2 large egg yolks
- 2 tablespoons cornstarch

Instructions:

1. **Whisk Ingredients:** Whisk together milk, sugar, peanut butter, egg yolks, and cornstarch in a saucepan.
2. **Cook:** Heat over medium heat, whisking constantly until thickened.
3. **Chill:** Refrigerate for 2 hours before serving.

Fig Pudding

Ingredients:

- 2 cups (480ml) whole milk
- 1 cup (150g) fresh figs, chopped
- ¼ cup (50g) sugar
- 2 tablespoons cornstarch
- 1 teaspoon vanilla extract

Instructions:

1. **Cook Figs:** In a saucepan, cook figs with sugar and a little water until soft.
2. **Prepare Custard:** Whisk together milk and cornstarch, then add to the figs.
3. **Cook:** Heat over medium heat until thickened.
4. **Chill:** Stir in vanilla and refrigerate for 2 hours before serving.

Carrot Cake Custard

Ingredients:

- 2 cups (480ml) whole milk
- 1 carrot, grated
- ¼ cup (50g) sugar
- 2 tablespoons cornstarch
- 1 teaspoon cinnamon
- 1 teaspoon vanilla extract

Instructions:

1. **Cook Carrot:** Simmer grated carrot with a little water until soft.
2. **Prepare Custard:** Whisk together milk, sugar, cornstarch, and cinnamon.
3. **Combine:** Add carrot mixture to custard and cook until thickened.
4. **Chill:** Stir in vanilla and refrigerate for 2 hours.

Apple Cinnamon Pudding

Ingredients:

- 2 cups (480ml) whole milk
- 1 apple, peeled and diced
- ½ cup (100g) sugar
- 1 teaspoon cinnamon
- 2 tablespoons cornstarch
- 1 teaspoon vanilla extract

Instructions:

1. **Cook Apple:** Simmer diced apple with sugar and a little water until soft.
2. **Prepare Custard:** Whisk together milk, cinnamon, and cornstarch, then add to the apple mixture.
3. **Cook:** Heat over medium heat, stirring constantly until thickened.
4. **Chill:** Stir in vanilla and refrigerate for 2 hours before serving.

Cinnamon Custard

Ingredients:

- 2 cups (480ml) whole milk
- ¼ cup (50g) sugar
- 2 tablespoons cornstarch
- 1 teaspoon cinnamon
- 1 teaspoon vanilla extract
- 2 large egg yolks

Instructions:

1. **Mix Ingredients:** Whisk together milk, sugar, cinnamon, and cornstarch in a saucepan.
2. **Cook:** Heat over medium heat, stirring constantly until thickened.
3. **Add Egg Yolks:** Slowly whisk in egg yolks and cook until thickened.
4. **Chill:** Stir in vanilla and refrigerate for 2 hours before serving.

Banana Custard

Ingredients:

- 2 cups (480ml) whole milk
- ½ cup (100g) sugar
- 2 tablespoons cornstarch
- 1 ripe banana, mashed
- 2 large egg yolks
- 1 teaspoon vanilla extract

Instructions:

1. **Mix Ingredients:** Whisk together milk, sugar, cornstarch, and mashed banana in a saucepan.
2. **Cook:** Heat over medium heat, stirring constantly until thickened.
3. **Add Egg Yolks:** Slowly whisk in egg yolks and cook until thickened.
4. **Chill:** Stir in vanilla and refrigerate for 2 hours before serving.

Brown Sugar Custard

Ingredients:

- 2 cups (480ml) whole milk
- ½ cup (100g) brown sugar
- 2 tablespoons cornstarch
- 2 large egg yolks
- 1 teaspoon vanilla extract

Instructions:

1. **Mix Ingredients:** Whisk together milk, brown sugar, and cornstarch in a saucepan.
2. **Cook:** Heat over medium heat, stirring constantly until thickened.
3. **Add Egg Yolks:** Slowly whisk in egg yolks and cook until thickened.
4. **Chill:** Stir in vanilla and refrigerate for 2 hours before serving.

Chocolate Mint Pudding

Ingredients:

- 2 cups (480ml) whole milk
- ¼ cup (50g) sugar
- ¼ cup (25g) unsweetened cocoa powder
- 2 tablespoons cornstarch
- ½ teaspoon peppermint extract
- 2 large egg yolks

Instructions:

1. **Mix Ingredients:** Whisk together milk, sugar, cocoa powder, and cornstarch in a saucepan.
2. **Cook:** Heat over medium heat, stirring constantly until thickened.
3. **Add Egg Yolks:** Slowly whisk in egg yolks and cook until thickened.
4. **Flavor:** Stir in peppermint extract and refrigerate for 2 hours before serving.

Raspberry Custard

Ingredients:

- 2 cups (480ml) whole milk
- 1 cup (150g) fresh raspberries, pureed
- ¼ cup (50g) sugar
- 2 tablespoons cornstarch
- 2 large egg yolks
- 1 teaspoon vanilla extract

Instructions:

1. **Prepare Raspberry Puree:** Blend raspberries until smooth, then strain to remove seeds.
2. **Mix Ingredients:** Whisk together milk, sugar, cornstarch, and raspberry puree in a saucepan.
3. **Cook:** Heat over medium heat, stirring constantly until thickened.
4. **Add Egg Yolks:** Slowly whisk in egg yolks and cook until thickened.
5. **Chill:** Stir in vanilla and refrigerate for 2 hours before serving.

Coconut Mango Pudding

Ingredients:

- 1 cup (240ml) coconut milk
- 1 cup (240ml) whole milk
- 1 cup (150g) fresh mango puree
- ¼ cup (50g) sugar
- 2 tablespoons cornstarch
- 1 teaspoon vanilla extract

Instructions:

1. **Mix Ingredients:** Whisk together coconut milk, whole milk, sugar, and cornstarch in a saucepan.
2. **Cook:** Heat over medium heat, stirring constantly until thickened.
3. **Add Mango Puree:** Stir in mango puree and cook for another 2-3 minutes.
4. **Chill:** Remove from heat, stir in vanilla, and refrigerate for 2 hours before serving.

www.ingramcontent.com/pod-product-compliance
Lightning Source LLC
LaVergne TN
LVHW081501060526
838201LV00056BA/2876